AFFILIATE MARKETING SECRETS YOU ARE NOT SUPPOSED TO KNOW

Proven Tips and Strategies You Can Use To Start and Grow a Profitable Affiliate Marketing Business Even As A Complete Beginner Starting Today

STEPHAN GREY

Stephan Grey

Copyright ©2022 Stephan Grey

All Rights Reserved

Affiliate Marketing Secrets You Are Not Supposed to Know

INTRODUCTION

Do you want to discover how to make a lot of money with affiliate marketing in even if you're a complete beginner?

CHAPTER 1

What is Affiliate Marketing, anyway?
How Does Affiliate Marketing work?

CHAPTER 2

Moving through the Various Stages of Your Affiliate Marketing System
Which affiliate marketing niches are the most profitable?

CHAPTER 3

How to Choose a Product to Promote

CHAPTER 4

6 Questions You Must Answer Correctly To Promote A Product Effectively As An Affiliate

CHAPTER 5

Making sales is a numbers game.

CHAPTER 6

You and Your List

Chapter 7

What is the Difference Between WhatsApp Marketing and Email Marketing?

Chapter 8

The Power of Making Offers

Chapter 9

18 Tips to help you increase the profitability of your advertising, conversions and sales

Conclusion

Affiliate Marketing Secrets You Are Not Supposed to Know

INTRODUCTION

Do you want to discover how to make a lot of money with affiliate marketing in even if you're a complete beginner?

Who hasn't sold something on the internet before?

If you said yes, you are the reason I wrote this book.

In the next eight chapters of this book, you'll learn about growing a seven-figure online business by recommending other people's products/services.

I decided to write this book because I believe this is an issue that needs to be addressed.

The term "affiliate marketing" is clearly misunderstood by many individuals.

If you type "affiliate marketing" into Google, you'll get a lot of results.

People do all sorts of thing and tag it as affiliate marketing.

That's why I decided to write a complete Book on the Subject in question

Affiliate Marketing Secrets You Are Not Supposed to Know

I'm going to break it down in such a way that even a two-year-old will be able to comprehend and apply the information that I'll be providing.

So, if you're ready to embark on this thrilling adventure with me then fasten your seat belt and Let's get started in the world of Affiliate Marketing.

CHAPTER 1

What is Affiliate Marketing, anyway?

Before I get into what affiliate marketing is and isn't, I think I should explain what affiliate marketing isn't.

1. Affiliate marketing is not a Ponzi scheme or a get-rich-quick scheme.

Many individuals, particularly on this side of the Continent, have been conditioned to seek out free money.

They want a plug-and-play system where they can just put their money in, go to bed, and wake up to massive earnings.

As a result, many people would continue to fall prey to various ponzi schemes.

If there is one thing I've learned in my over 5 years of internet marketing, it's that there is no such thing as free money.

You can't reap what and where you didn't plant.

Read it again *slowly this time around.*

You can't reap what and where you didn't plant!

So, if you consider Affiliate Marketing to be a get-rich-quick plan, this is not for you.

Take a look next door.

2. Affiliate marketing and network marketing are not the same thing.

This is another area where I see a lot of individuals getting things mixed up and making mistakes.

"Bring one person, bring two people" has nothing to do with affiliate marketing.

Affiliate marketing and network marketing are two different creatures.

They may resemble each other, but they are not the same thing.

What is Affiliate Marketing, exactly?

Affiliate marketing, simply described, is the promotion of a person's or company's product or service in exchange for a commission.

That's all there is to it.

How Does Affiliate Marketing work?

It simply works by Recommending to others high-value digital products created by top specialists that are valuable and assist them in solving various challenges.

E.g: So, if you're marketing a product that teaches you (how to lose weight in 30 days without exercising) and it costs $49, the Affiliate network / product owner might pay you as much as $25 on each sale you make.

You can easily utilize social media, such as WhatsApp and Email marketing, to run promotions

(I'll go through how to do that later in this book), and you'll earn a commission when people buy.

It's that simple.

One of the things I like about affiliate marketing is that you don't have to deal with all of the problems that come with coming up with an information product because the products in question aren't yours.

Some of these issues include:

=>creating a website

=>setting up your product sales page

=>customer support

=>managing employees

=>constant product content updating... and so on.

All of those things will be taken care of by the product vendor; all you have to do is promote it.

You must comprehend this if you want to become a successful and productive affiliate marketer.

As an affiliate marketer, it is your obligation to offer **HELPFUL** items to **PEOPLE WHO NEED THEM** (are interested in them) and can afford them.

And you accomplish this by:

a. Developing a product that addresses a problem that affects a group of people.

b. Attracting a big number of people who are interested in and eager to solve the problem, as well as those who can buy the product. (It's critical not to try to sell to those who are bankrupt.)

c. Establishing yourself as someone they like, respect, and trust. (a dependable advisor) It is a well-known reality that individuals prefer to buy from people they know, like, or trust. Whatever you do, keep the (KLT) Factor in mind.

d. Creating and distributing very compelling messages to them via email, Facebook, Instagram, and other channels to make them see reasons why they need that product.

The goal is for them to understand why the product/service you're suggesting will benefit them.

People are always tuned in to WIIFM, which is something you should keep in mind. **(Can you tell me What's In It For Me?)**

If you can't persuade them that the product or service will benefit them, you're going to have a tough time selling it.

I want you to read and re-read this chapter until you understand all you've just read.

In the following chapter, I'll go through the stages of your Affiliate Marketing System, as well as the best Evergreen niches to promote products in and much more.

Affiliate Marketing Secrets You Are Not Supposed to Know

Chapter 2

Moving through the Various Stages of Your Affiliate Marketing System

So, in the first chapter of this book, I gave a quick overview of affiliate marketing, including how it works and how to benefit from it.

You should think of it as recommending useful Items or services to individuals who need them and can afford them, like I indicated.

The truth is that we're all affiliate marketers; the only difference is that we don't all get paid for recommending products to others.

For example, I'm sure that at some point in the past, someone bought a phone, a garment, a drink, or even a specific brand of automobile just because they saw you using it or because you recommended it to someone because of a friend or relative who was using it.

What you just accomplished is known as Affiliate Marketing, *in case you didn't know.*

Were you compensated for making that Recomendation?

Maybe you were, but it's more than likely that you didn't.

That is why I want you to be intentional about it and look for methods to be compensated for recommending a product or service to others.

In coming chapters, I'll go through this in greater detail.

So, let's speak about the many stages of a successful affiliate marketing system and what you should promote as an affiliate marketer.

1. The first step is to choose a product

This is where you register for the affiliate program or platform that you want to use to market their products or services.

2. The Stage of the Marketing Funnel

Here you will create the marketing funnel that will be utilized to sell the product.

3. Getting quality Traffic.

This is the point at which you begin directing traffic to the marketing funnel you developed in stage. 2

If nobody sees the product you are promoting then you won't make any money that is why getting people who have money to spend and are interested in what you are promoting is very very important.

So next, we'll look at how to choose a hot product to market.

Which affiliate marketing niches are the most profitable?

Typically, if you want to start making a lot of money as an affiliate really fast, you should choose a product that is related to one of the four categories stated below, as these are considered evergreen markets.

-Finances, Business, Making Money, Investing

-Beauty and health

-Sexuality, Dating, and Relationships.

Secondly, choose a product that gives out substantial commissions.

An excellent place to start is with a product that pays at least 40% commissions and higher.

That is why I always advise beginning with digital products, because they pay the largest commissions to affiliates

The reason why digital products pay higher commissions is because there is usually no cost involved in printing or sending the product to the buyer as you have in physical products. It is usually available for instant download after payment.

All of this may appear complicated and time-consuming, but trust me when I say it isn't.

All that is required is commitment and a desire to put in the effort.

To get started, all you have to do is focus on your Affiliate marketing revenue goal, be deliberate about doing only the things that will help you get closer to your goal, and you'll have the strength and motivation to do what you need to do to succeed.

Chapter 3

How to Choose a Product to Promote

In this chapter, I'll elaborate on one of the points I made in the previous chapter, namely, selecting a product to promote.

There are numerous factors to consider when deciding what to promote.

You must consider the following:

1. The category in which the product belongs:

As I previously indicated, you should promote products in the make money online, health/beauty, relationship/sexuality, and travel niches because they are evergreen categories.

2. How useful is the content of the product?

This can be determined by looking at the number of positive reviews the product has received.

3. How Much Does the Product Pay in Commissions?

As I previously stated, if you want to make money quickly, you should start with marketing digital products, as they tend to pay the greatest commissions.

Please don't promote/recommend shady products simply because they pay well.

Remember, it's all about your reputation.

Protect it as if your life depended on it.

To get started as an affiliate, you can join one of two major types of internet affiliate systems.

(1) Robust Affiliate Networks (Robust Affiliate Networks):
This is the most important one.

To truly succeed as an affiliate, you must have access to a variety of products to promote, and there is no better way to do so than by joining a reputable affiliate network.

These affiliate networks include websites such as **Clickbank, Moreniche, Jvzoo, Share A Sale, Expertnaire** and others, which feature thousands of merchants.

Once you've joined the network, you'll have access to a variety of products that you can market.

(2) Affiliate Programs Created In-House:

There are a lot of businesses who have their own affiliate programs.

This implies that the affiliate program is limited to their own products.

The Amazon affiliate program works in this manner.

Most websites offer affiliate programs that you may join to sell their products if you look at the bottom links of their pages.

Systeme and **Getresponse**, for example, have their own affiliate programs.

Note: If you want to be a successful Affiliate Marketer, you must be more interested in addressing your prospect's problem than just getting a sale.

"No one gives a hoot about how much you know unless they know how much you truly care,".

That is correct.

When someone likes and trusts you, it becomes easier for them to part with their money for the product you're recommending since they believe it will solve their problem.

One more thing: I notice a lot of newcomers make this error when they first start out in affiliate marketing.

What is the hottest product to market on Clickbank, you hear people ask?

The truth is that majority of the Products on Clickbank hot products

The products you should choose and recommend to your audience will be determined by your audience.

For example, if you have a target audience interested in making money, it would be silly to promote weight loss items to them, even if they do need to lose weight.

It is a well-known reality that people would rather pay for what they want rather than what they require/need.

Let me repeat that statement once more.

People would prefer pay for what they want rather than what they require/need.

You will no longer struggle to make sales if you have this in the back of your mind, because you will continue to smile to the bank.

Chapter 4

6 Questions You Must Answer Correctly To Promote A Product Effectively As An Affiliate

The truth is that you need to have a dependable strategy in place if you want to achieve consistent sales.

You can make this system as easy or as complicated as you desire.

It's your option; however I like the basic method because I'm often lazy. Lol

Anyway, I'd want to offer you a six-step technique that I learned from my mentor, Toyin Omotoso that will help you simplify the process of choosing and promoting a product as an affiliate.

(1) What is the product I'm trying to sell?

(2) What is the product's benefit?

(3) Who is the product's potential buyer? Give specific examples.

(4) What is it that he desires?

(5) Where and how will I be able to get enough of them?

(6) What can I say to get their attention?

Now, let's look at how I may apply it to Fictitious PayPal report For Nigerians.

(1) What is the product I'm trying to sell?

A report on how to open a Paypal account in Nigeria, for instance.

(2) What is the product's advantage?

It enables you to create a verified PayPal account that allows you to send and receive money in Nigeria without having to change your IP address.

(3) Who is the product's potential buyer? Give specific examples.

a. Online freelancers who are having difficulty getting paid.

b. If another buyer audience exists, list it here.

(4) What is it that he desires?

He wants a secure PayPal account that he can use to send and receive money from individuals all around the world without worrying about PayPal stealing his funds.

(5) Where and how will I be able to get enough of them?

Targeting these audiences (those who like Udemy, Fiverr, etc.) with Facebook advertising

(6) What can I say to get their attention?

Have you been trying to register a Paypal account in Nigeria to send and receive money? I've got awesome news for you.

So tell me, was it really that difficult?

Affiliate Marketing Secrets You Are Not Supposed to Know

Chapter 5

Making sales is a numbers game.

In case you weren't aware. Making sales is a numbers game.

What exactly do I mean?

It's straightforward.

More individuals need to view your offer for the more sales you wish to make.

Isn't that reasonable?

I'm going to talk about some basic math here to help understand my point.

Assume you're running a paid Facebook ad with the following components in your sales funnel:

AD=> Optin Page = Thank you page => Offer

This is what the preceding means:

AD: What your subscriber sees before clicking for more information.

Optin page: This is the page where people enter their email address in exchange for the vital information you are providing.

After they've opted in, they'll be taken to a **thank you page** where they'll be provided further information about your offer.

Let's look at an example of what you might get if you complete everything correctly.

Assume you get **2500** clicks on your ad.

The cost per click is $0.5.

Optin rate = 34% (34/100) multiplied by 2500 = 850 optins

$1 is the cost per opt-in.

You have a **2 percent offer conversion rate**

$45 is the offer compensation (This is the affiliate commission per sale)

$250 is the amount spent on running AD.

2/100 x 850 = 17 (this means you made 17 sales)

17 × $45 =$756

After deducting the $250 spent on advertising, you have a profit of $500.

Can you see what I mean when I say that selling is a numbers game?

What should you do if you want to double your earnings?

You do that by showing your offer to more people by increasing your ad budget

You may boost your efforts by leveraging social media and employing attraction marketing to lure people to you, and then closing the sale on platforms like WhatsApp.

Before I wrap up this chapter, there's one more thing I'd want to mention.

You'll need to create a list if you want to make serious money with affiliate marketing. (I cannot emphasize this enough.) Your list might be an email marketing list or a WhatsApp group. etc

You must nurture your list to the point that they know, like, and trust you.

According to a survey, the average individual needs to see your offer at least seven times before taking action.

This implies you need to have your prospects on a list so you can connect with them frequently and feed their emotional bank accounts. Over time, a number of them will open up to you and buy the products and services you're recommending.

If you don't already have an email list, the first thing you need to do is set up an auto-responder or email marketing account.

There are a lot of them out there, but I recommend **Getresponse** if you want to market digital products.

They currently offer a forever FREE Plan and you can create an account using this link.

Chapter 6

You and Your List

I discussed how to make a lot of sales with affiliate marketing in the previous chapter, and one of the essential components is having a list.

It's possible that your list will be an email list or perhaps a WhatsApp group. It makes no difference.

What counts is that you have a set of people to whom you give useful information to on a regular basis and to whom you then advertise your offer.

If you haven't started building an email list yet, **Getresponse** and **Systeme.io** currently offers a forever **FREE** Plan .

With that said, I'd like to discuss three things that will help you raise your email open rate, which means more people will notice your offer and, as a result, your sales.

I have a question for you if you are already familiar with email marketing and how it works.

Are you fed up with receiving low email open rates every time you send a newsletter to your subscribers?

You should read this if you said yes.

Here are three strategies to increase your open rates and get more people to respond positively to your emails (guaranteed!)

1. Confirm that your emails are not being sent to the majority of your subscribers' spam folders.

This can be accomplished by verifying the spam score of your emails before sending them.

If you're unfamiliar with the term "spam score," let me explain.

This score is typically assigned to your email depending on the message's content and title.

It's a number between 1 and 10 on a scale of 1 to 10.

As a result, if your email contains phrases that email service providers such as Google and Yahoo deem spam words; your email will receive a higher spam score.

The higher the spam score, the more likely your emails will be forwarded to your subscribers' spam folders rather than their inboxes.

You can also use online spam testing services like https://mail-tester.com to send a preview copy of your email.

This will assist you in identifying issues with your email content or your email client in general. (Don't overlook this!)

Many people overlook this step and then wonder why their emails receive such a low open rate.

2. Double-check that your emails aren't ending up in the Promotions Folder of the vast majority of your subscribers.

The truth is that, after the spam folder, the promotions folder is the second worst location for your emails to end up.

Because, in my experience, email service companies such as Gmail have a way of categorizing any email you send based on the content of the message.

If your email contains many instances of phrases such as **"sell," "buy," "pay," "money," "cash," "marketing," "order," "finance," "shop," "business,"** and so on, it's a red flag.

Alternatively, if your email contains too many links in the body, it is likely to be put to the promotions folder, which will impact your open rates.

The truth is that not everyone goes to their Gmail promotion folder to hunt for emails, which is why you should keep this in mind when writing your email message and make sure it isn't too "salesy."

3. Use headlines that are CURIOSITY Driven

"CURIOSITY" is our middle name as humans, therefore when you utilize headlines that pique your subscribers' interest, it's only natural for them to open and read the substance of your emails.

"Curiosity killed the cat," as the cliché goes.

Humans, it turns out, are also driven by curiosity.

Simply make sure the email content is worthwhile, or else you'll be training them to ignore future emails or perhaps unsubscribe from your list.

If you found this chapter useful, you'll be interested to know that there is a Digital Marketing Course I recommend called 72IG Implementation Program which includes a full module dedicated to performing email marketing correctly.

Mastering email marketing is just one of the many factors that will turn you into an unstoppable digital marketer, and the 72IG training will provide you with everything you need to get started.

Affiliate Marketing Secrets You Are Not Supposed to Know

Chapter 7

What is the Difference Between WhatsApp Marketing and Email Marketing?

There has been a long-running argument about which of them is the most effective.

Some argue that WhatsApp is more potent, while others argue that email marketing is still the best option.

Well, here's the thing: I believe the two may be utilized together, and based on the type of goods you're selling, you can choose which is more appropriate.

Many individuals have asked me for my thoughts on WhatsApp and email marketing.

They want to know which channel is the most effective for generating daily sales.

So, here's my take on the situation.

To begin, I'd want to state that I feel both are effective marketing tactics.

Personally, I favor a combination of the two.

However, I have discovered that WhatsApp is more user-friendly for those who are new to internet marketing.

WhatsApp is a great tool for converting strangers into clients.

The WhatsApp messenger functions similarly to a friend-to-friend app.

It's primarily used for one-on-one conversations.

Because individuals may utilize it to contact you one-on-one, it acts as a form of word-of-mouth marketing, allowing you to quickly establish TRUST.

WhatsApp also allows you to send broadcast messages, however I believe this is limited to 300 messages per broadcast list or something similar.

WhatsApp can also be used to market to a group of people.

However, the number of participants in a WhatsApp group is extremely limited.

To accommodate more members, you'll need to create multiple groups.

Because of the restrictions on broadcasts and group members, it's tough to use it to grow a business unless your products are high-ticket items (e.g. real estate, cars, luxury)

When you know how to use email marketing, it can be incredibly effective.

Many affiliates, I've noticed, simply don't know how to prosper with it.

When I execute a campaign, I produce tens of thousands of leads.

I'm talking about around 2000 leads per day.

I'm not going to be able to respond to them over WhatsApp.

It'll just be a waste of time.

Instead, I add them to a mailing list so that my Autoresponder may send them follow-up emails.

These follow-up messages assist me in extracting the serious ones to WhatsApp, where they can be closed more easily.

This means that instead of the initial 2000 leads, I'll only have to talk to a few people (maybe 200).

So, here's what I've come to.

(1) If possible, combine WhatsApp and Email marketing.

You start by getting folks on your email list, and then select the best of them to join your WhatsApp list.

(2) If you don't have enough power to handle all of the back-and-forth on WhatsApp, concentrate on email marketing and become an expert at it.

(3) However, if you are unable to use email, concentrate on WhatsApp marketing for the time being and master it.

That is my recommendation.

By the way, both channels may be used to sell nearly anything, including apparel, food, electronics, and digital goods.

However, I will prefer to use WhatsApp for high-priced products (that pay me at least $8,000 on each sale) because it helps you develop trust quickly."

I hope you got something out of this chapter because it is jam-packed with useful information.

You might want to go back and reread it several times.

Chapter 8

The Power of Making Offers

The main difference between a typical marketer and one who understands human psychology is that the former sells products, whilst the latter sells offers.

A product or service is only one component of a package deal.

When you learn how to make offers, your life will change forever because you will no longer fight to generate sales since people will be asking you to collect their money all over the place.

People are more likely to buy from you if they believe they are being ripped off, even if your pricing is higher, than if they believe you are ripping them off, even if your price is lower.

It's an odd behavior.

In his new book, How to Sell to Nigerians, Akin Alabi explains the power of offers.

If you don't already own a copy of the book, I strongly advise you to do so as soon as possible.

He told the story of wanting to buy a property in Lekki Nigeria a few years ago in the book.

He was left with two options.

2. N120m and N115m

But, despite the fact that the house was valued at N120 million, he eventually purchased it since the seller made him an incredible offer.

", He claimed "He would be liable for rectifying any issue in the house within a year of purchasing it.

And if it's a structural flaw, he'll give a refund."

The individual with the N120 million offer won because of this modest offer.

And the second man was defeated.

The point of these two stories isn't to teach you about price.

Pricing is something else entirely, and it is outside the scope of this chapter.

The major takeaway here is to anticipate what your clients will desire in order to make them satisfied and confident with their purchase.

You should also look for ways to make the product you're marketing more valuable as an Affiliate Marketer, which you can accomplish by looking for incentives to add to it.

Here's the deal: Hundreds, if not thousands, of other affiliates are likely to be promoting the same product you are, so you must find a way to stand out.

Begin by asking yourself, "What can I do to attract people to buy from me or what bonuses can I add to this product to make it more valuable and, as a result, draw more prospects to buy with my affiliate link?"

There's one more thing you should be aware of when it comes to making proposals.

Bonuses should be relevant to the product you're offering.

"You can't bags of rice and give cement as a bonus,"

Soft drinks, wine, and chicken, etc. should be your bonuses."

Always double-check that any bonus you're offering is relevant/complimentary to the product you're marketing.

Affiliate Marketing Secrets You Are Not Supposed to Know

Chapter 9

18 Tips to help you increase the profitability of your advertising, conversions and sales

Here are 18 Tips to help you increase the profitability of your advertising, increase conversions, and increase sales:

1. The first tip is to Use lead magnet.

People are addicted to free things, whether it's a free class, e-book, webinar, or 15-minute walkthrough session.

Make use of it.

However, be sure that anything you're giving away is directly related to what you're attempting to promote.

You also don't have to bury your lead magnet offer in the body of your article while creating it.

Ads with the lead magnet offer prominently displayed perform better

Keep in mind that people adore getting something for nothing.

However, it is preferable if they are informed ahead of time.

2. Be realistic in your Projections/Expectation

On average, one out of every ten people who see what you're selling purchases it right away.

It's possible that it'll be even less.

Maybe like 1 in every 100 people

So Patience is a must.

Nurture and follow-up are essential.

3. One common blunder is putting so much effort into the media (photo or video) for an advertisement and then neglecting the ad copy.

You should make sure that your sales content is just as effective as the image or video in your ad.

Your remarks should enlarge/highlight/embellish the image or video you've created

Nothing should be left to chance.

4. Combine paid and organic promotions at some point.

Organic traffic is potent and compounds beautifully, despite its slowness. Paid traffic is quick and helps you grow a list rapidly.

If you combine the two, you'll give your company a huge boost.

5. Include exclusive offers and promotions on a regular basis.

Is there a Christmas discount?

Is there a weekend discount?

Is there a TGIF discount?

Is there a Black Friday deal?

Or Maybe a Discount for New Year's Resolutions?

Is there a discount for Sallah?

Is there a discount at the end of the month.

Carry them out.

However, be sure the math makes logical. Don't throw away all of your profits in order to increase sales.

6. Experiment with different ad setups, presells, and angles.

"Cast your bread in six or seven directions onto the waves, for you never know which will be profitable."

As the Holy Book declares.

7. Retest, retreat, and revise on a regular basis.

The conventional wisdom is that if something is functioning, you should milk it until it stops working.

Excellent advice.

If something is working, a better choice is to seek out methods to improve it while it continues to work in the background.

It's possible that your present ad is effective. But what if you could improve on it?

8. Don't forget to market what you do/sell at every chance.

Everywhere you look, there's an opportunity to sell something.

Be the man that doesn't hold back when it comes to their business.

After all, if you don't have a business, you don't have a business.

9. Make an effort with your advertisements.

Are you here to make money or to have a good time?

Take it all the way.

Winners don't take half measures.

It's 100% or none at all!

10. Language has a great deal of power.

One person says, "Get this product for 20% off." Another person says, "Get this goods for $20 discount,"

They both uttered the same thing at the same time.

Who, on the other hand, do you believe would get better results?

11. Your ad must be one-of-a-kind and beneficial. But most importantly, it must be specific.

You didn't save up money to run ads just to have fun. Act as if you're trying to make money.

12. Use other people's networks to your advantage

What exactly is influencer marketing?

Friends with a sizable following? Yes.

Church? Yes

What about school clubs and associations? Yes.

You can sell just about everywhere.

13. You must master the art of giving things away. You won't be able to grow if you try to keep everything.

Giving some to gain more is the basic premise of advertising.

14. Keep in mind that you're in the business of direct response marketing.

Every action leads to a sale, or at the very least a future sale.

You're not a multibillion-dollar corporation with unlimited advertising budgets.

You lose if you snooze.

15. If you want to be a successful affiliate for any product, either ask for testimonials from the product owner or make your own testimonial folder.

The best form of marketing is customer success.

Make use of it.

It's worth milking.

16. Have an unhealthy obsession with traffic.

You can't save souls in a church that's empty.

Every day, every hour, and every minute, you must continually drive people into your funnel.

That's how you get the job done.

17. Experiment with different sources of traffic

-WhatsApp?

-Quora?

-Pinterest?

-Snapchat?

-TikTok?

You never know what you'll come across.

18. People with shut mouths don't get fed.

There's a concept known as a friendzone.

Even though you want more from them, someone you like puts you in that awful zone.

Do you believe that friendzoning occurs only in friendships and love relationships?

Obviously not.

Your audience/list may decide to unfriend you.

They begin to regard you as an entertainer who offers enthralling stories over time...

Or a teacher who is constantly handing out freebies.

And by the time you ask for a sale, they'll be hesitant to hand over their cash.

But it's not because they don't believe you're valuable.

But that's because they're accustomed to receiving it for free.

People enjoy discussing the concept of 'providing value.'

But where does providing value end and selling begin?

You need to make a profit. That is why you are in business.

Affiliate Marketing Secrets You Are Not Supposed to Know

Conclusion

While Affiliate marketing can be a very rewarding business to engage in, it does require knowledge in copywriting, storytelling ability to run paid ads to scale up your business as well as knowing how to make powerful offers.

I really do hope you got value and enjoyed reading this material just as I have enjoyed writing it.

So now is the time to go out there and win.

I wish you all the best.

Made in the USA
Coppell, TX
07 June 2022

78582653R00038